Where the North Pole?

by Megan Stine

illustrated by Robert Squier

Penguin Workshop

For Jane Stine, Jane O'Connor, and Jenny Fanelli,
preeminent among the many great women editors
who shepherded my books over the years. And for
Bill and Cody, who watched me write them—MS

For my brother Donald, a polar
explorer in his own right—RS

PENGUIN WORKSHOP
An imprint of Penguin Random House LLC, New York

First published in the United States of America by Penguin Workshop,
an imprint of Penguin Random House LLC, New York, 2022

Visit us online at penguinrandomhouse.com.

Library of Congress Cataloging-in-Publication Data is available.

Printed in the United States of America

ISBN 9780593093245 (paperback)   10 9 8 7 6 5 4 3 2   WOR
ISBN 9780593093252 (library binding)   10 9 8 7 6 5 4 3 2 1 WOR

Contents

Where Is the North Pole?

Robert E. Peary had wanted one thing in life—fame. He was born in Pennsylvania in 1856. Since childhood, he had dreamed about reaching the North Pole. In the late 1890s, most of the world had already been explored by Europeans and Americans. But no one had ever reached the North Pole—not on foot or by boat. Not even the Indigenous people who lived in the Arctic had ever dared to go that far north.

No one knew what the North Pole would be like if they ever reached it. Was it land? Was it ice? Was it water? Many people thought there was a so-called Open Polar Sea, with nothing but water at the top of the globe. Other people thought Greenland—a huge island country in the Arctic—might reach all the way to the North Pole. Maybe they could find it by just walking north.

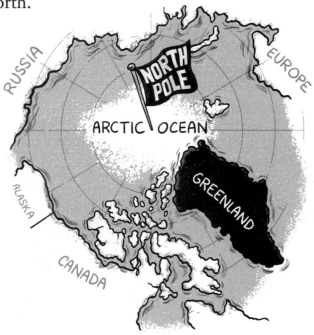

Robert Peary knew that finding the North Pole would make him famous. But he had no idea how hard it would be.

He would have to travel to the northwestern shores of Greenland by ship and be dropped there to camp for a long, dark winter. With no way to get home for a whole year, he would have to learn how to survive in the Arctic cold. He would have to hunt and kill seals, polar bears, and musk oxen—or starve if he couldn't find any. He would have to learn how to drive a pack of nearly wild dogs pulling long sleds loaded with supplies. He would have to walk for hundreds of miles across the ice, in blinding snowstorms.

Sometimes the temperatures would drop to fifty degrees below zero. It would get so cold that Peary's dogs' feet and tails would freeze into the snow. The ice would have to be chopped away to free the dogs. In the brutal cold, Peary's own toes would become so frostbitten, they would snap and break off! From then on, he could only shuffle as he walked. When food was gone, he would get so hungry that he'd eat his own dogs to survive!

Peary didn't know any of this when he first set sail to find the North Pole in 1891. He also didn't know that one man who came along on the trip would become his biggest rival—seeking to reach the North Pole on his own.

Would either man ever reach the pole and return alive?

And what terrible things would one of them do to achieve the fame he had craved?

CHAPTER 1
The Arctic Circle

The North Pole is a single point at the "top" of the earth. It is the point farthest north on the globe. (The South Pole is the single point at the "bottom" of the earth.) The North Pole is also at the exact center of what is called the Arctic Circle—a huge area of ice and water.

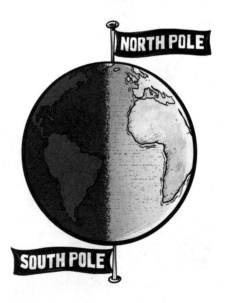

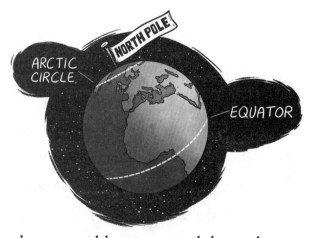

Look at a world map or a globe and you will see horizontal lines drawn on it. The line that goes around the very middle of the earth, like a belt, is called the equator. The Arctic Circle is marked by the line near the top of the globe and includes the whole frozen area around the North Pole. The distance from the most southern points of the Arctic Circle to the North Pole is about 1,600 miles.

The Arctic Circle is huge—over five and a half million square miles in area. That's much bigger than the United States. It's even bigger than China and Mexico put together!

Who Owns the North Pole?

This map of the Arctic Circle shows a view of the earth looking down on the globe, with the North Pole at the center. Eight countries have land that reaches into the Arctic Circle—Norway, Sweden, Finland, Russia, Greenland (which is a special part of Denmark), Iceland, the United States, and Canada.

But does anyone own the North Pole? No. The North Pole is like the oceans—open to anyone. You don't need a passport to go visit the North Pole.

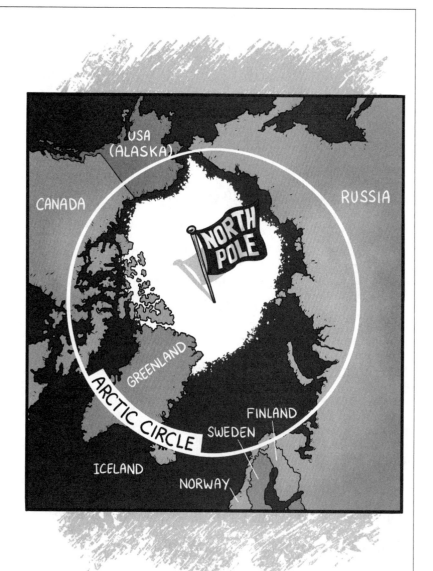

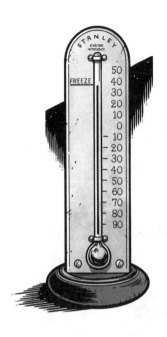

The Arctic Circle is one of the coldest places on the earth. In summer, the average temperature is only fifty degrees Fahrenheit. In winter, it can reach ninety degrees below zero in some parts of the Arctic Circle.

Almost the entire Arctic Circle is water, which is frozen much of the year. Frozen seawater is called sea ice. It's about nine feet thick, but can be as thick as fifteen feet. Throughout the year, the sea ice melts and then freezes again. Huge chunks of sea ice break apart, letting rivers and lakes of seawater flow between them. The ice floes drift apart. It can be impossible to walk straight to the North Pole without crossing water at some point—or waiting for the ice to form again.

Some parts of the Arctic Circle do include solid land. The three largest land areas belong to Greenland, Russia, and Canada. Which country has the smallest area in the Arctic Circle? Iceland!

Greenland and Iceland—Two Mixed-Up Names

Greenland is barely green at all, with very few plants and almost no trees. It's almost all ice! Iceland, an island country nearby, is the opposite. It has mostly green rolling hills and a lot less ice.

How did these two countries get such wrong names?

Greenland was named by an explorer, Erik the Red. He had been sent there from Iceland as

Greenland

punishment for a crime he'd committed. When he finally returned home, he told everyone that he had found a beautiful place to settle. But he may not have been telling the truth about this new land. He may have named it Greenland so people would want to live there.

No one knows for sure how Iceland got its name. One story is that the first settlers saw ice along the coastline and named the country before they realized that it was mostly green and beautiful.

Iceland

In the Arctic, even solid land is mostly covered in ice or snow. Most of Greenland is covered in an ice sheet, much thicker than sea ice. In the center of Greenland, the sheet is almost two miles thick! When it snows in Greenland, the snow packs down and becomes ice, so the sheet gets thicker. Chunks of the ice sheet break off near the coast. They become dangerous icebergs that float out to sea.

The Arctic Circle is sometimes called the "Land of the Midnight Sun." Why? Because, depending on how far north in the Arctic Circle you are, the sun stays up for days, weeks, or months at a time. At the North Pole, smack in the middle of the Arctic Circle, the sun rises and sets only once a year! It comes up in March and stays up for six full months. Then the sun sets, and the North Pole is completely dark for six months of "polar nights." When explorers like Robert Peary searched for the pole, they had to travel in summer and get back to their base camp by fall, or else they would be marching across the ice in the dark.

Why does the sun set only once a year at the North Pole?

To understand the answer, you first have to think about why we see the sun "rise" and "set." The answer is that the earth is always spinning or turning. It makes one complete turn every twenty-four hours. The parts of the earth facing the sun have day. The parts facing away from the sun have night.

The earth spins around what we call its axis. This axis is like an imaginary "stick" going straight through it from the North Pole to the South Pole. But the stick does not stand up straight. It's tilted so that our planet spins at an angle.

At the same time the earth is spinning on its axis, it is also following a path (orbiting) around the sun. When the northern half of the earth is tilted toward the sun, it has summer—and there are six months of daylight at the North Pole. Later in the year, when the northern half of the earth is tilted away from the sun, the north has winter. Then there are six months of darkness at the North Pole.

When it's dark in the Arctic Circle, people sometimes see a brilliant light show called the "northern lights" or aurora borealis. The northern lights are flashes and streaks of colored light in the night sky. Mostly green, but sometimes purple, red, and blue, they spread across the dark sky in swirling patterns that are visible for miles. The auroras happen when particles from the sun enter the earth's atmosphere near the poles. They can be seen from almost anywhere in the Arctic, including Alaska. Amazingly, when the northern lights flash in the Arctic, the same thing happens at the South Pole—at the exact same time!

It's as if there are two identical light shows going on at the top and bottom of the earth.

The Arctic Circle—and especially the North Pole—was unknown to the Western world until the late 1890s. Americans and Europeans knew that a "north pole" existed. But they had no idea

what it would be like if they ever got there.

They did know one thing, though—
Indigenous peoples lived in the Arctic and knew
how to survive in that frozen land. Without their
help, no one from the outside world would ever
reach the North Pole.

CHAPTER 2
People of the Arctic

For thousands of years, people have lived in the Arctic. In Finland, Norway, Sweden, and Russia, there have long been Indigenous people called the Sami. They fish, hunt, and keep reindeer herds.

A Sami man and his reindeer

In Alaska, there are the Aleut people. They live on a string of islands off the western coast of Alaska that swoop across the Pacific Ocean to Russia.

However, the largest number of people native to the Arctic region are an ethnic group called the Inuit. The Inuit live in Greenland, Canada, and Alaska. Originally, they came from an ancient Alaskan people called the Thule. There are more than 150,000 Inuit living in those Arctic areas today.

An Inuit fishing in Greenland today

In the past—long before any other people ever explored the Arctic—the Inuit lived together in small family groups that wandered from place to place, searching for food.

In summer, they lived in tents made out of sealskins. In winter, they built large igloos near their coastal villages.

An igloo is a dome-shaped house made out of blocks of packed snow. With thick walls, the cold and wind stay outside so people can sleep inside and stay warm. Each igloo has only one opening or entrance. A block of snow is pushed into the opening to close it up from the inside. There must be a small hole to let air in, so people can breathe.

All the Inuit villages were near the coastline.
Why? Because if people traveled too far inland,
they wouldn't find much food.

Staying warm and finding food were the two
most important tasks for an Inuit family. Warm
clothing, boots, and sleeping bags could be made

from bearskins and sealskins. The Inuit ate a diet of mostly seals, whales, and fish. They hunted seals from the water's edge, or from kayaks, and hunted whales from larger, wider boats called umiaks. From whales they got food, and also whale oil, which they burned in small stone lamps inside their igloos and tents. They also hunted polar bears, walruses, musk oxen, Arctic foxes, and reindeer.

Dog sleds were an important part of Inuit life. The Inuit raised beautiful Arctic dogs. Some were bred from wolves. The dogs were used to pull sleds and haul large chunks of meat in winter.

They also protected the family groups from bears by barking when one was nearby.

Meat was eaten raw because it was hard to make a fire for cooking in a land of snow, ice, and not many trees. (Also the Inuit did not know about matches, which made it even harder to start a fire.)

There were almost no plants or vegetables for the Inuit to eat. But their diet of raw meat made up for it. How? Some raw meats contain quite a bit of vitamin C. So the Inuit diet kept them healthy.

Inuit people were relatively short. The men were only a little over five feet tall. The women were usually about five inches shorter. They also had small hands, feet, noses, and ears. Their physical makeup helped the Inuit to withstand the bitter cold. Smaller features made them less likely to suffer from frostbite. All Inuit people had long, dark hair. They let it fall over their faces in the cold, to keep them warmer.

Inuit men and women had excellent eyesight. They were used to living in darkness for long periods and could see well enough to sew or hunt in the dark.

The Inuit tribes spoke a number of different languages. In Canada, the most common Inuit language was Inuktitut. In Greenland, the Inuit spoke Kalaallisut. Today, most of these Indigenous people also speak English, Danish, or French.

Traditionally, the Inuit people divided the work. Men were the hunters and fishers. When someone killed a seal, everyone got to share it—even if they hadn't helped with the hunt. Women cleaned the animal skins and made clothes. To make clothing, Inuit women chewed the hairless side of the skins with their teeth! That softened up the skin so it would make a comfortable pair of pants, boots, or stockings.

The Inuit had different customs and rules about marriage. For one thing, some men had more than one wife. Husbands and wives sometimes switched partners, too.

Much of their time was spent finding food to stay alive. For good luck they carved small animal figures out of whalebone, antlers, or stone. When outsiders began to arrive in the Arctic, the Inuit began to carve larger sculptures to sell or trade with visitors.

In modern times, the Inuit have held on to many of their same customs. To hunt whales, the Inuit use harpoons. (There are laws restricting the number of whales that can be killed per year.) But many Inuit also use modern tools and weapons—rifles to hunt seals and polar bears. They buy clothing and kayaks from stores—they don't have to make them from animal skins. And they use snowmobiles instead of dogsleds.

Still, some Inuit, especially in the far north, stick to the old ways. They can be seen on the ice, driving dogsleds to hunt for seals and walruses. They are happy to take tourists for a dogsled ride, too. With luck, visitors might even catch a glimpse of the beautiful animals that share the frozen landscape with them.

CHAPTER 3
Where Polar Bears Rule the World

There are almost no animals living at the very top of the world—because there is almost nothing for them to eat. Once in a while, a polar bear will end up at the North Pole because it's been traveling on sea ice. A few seabirds have been spotted that far north. But most Arctic animals, birds, and fish live farther south. They live within the Arctic Circle, but closer to water and land where food is more plentiful.

At the top of the food chain is the beautiful, white furry polar bear. Standing up to ten feet tall on their hind legs, polar bears are among the largest bears in the world. Their skin underneath the fur is black. Their tongues are blue. Polar bear fur looks white—but it's actually colorless! It just looks white because it reflects light, the way snow and ice look white, even though they're made of clear water.

Polar bears' two layers of fur keep them warm on land, and that's where they spend most of their time. But fur alone is not thick enough to keep them warm in the freezing cold water. For that, they need a four-inch-thick layer of fat under their skin. The fat keeps them warm for the few minutes when they're swimming. Still, they usually stay in the water only a short time. To swim, polar bears use their front paws to paddle, and keep their back feet flat to steer. Each paw is about twelve inches across—the size of a dinner plate!

A polar bear's pawprint in the snow

To stay fat, polar bears eat mostly seals. Some Arctic seals, called ribbon seals, have beautiful black and white markings. Harp seals have white fur as babies, so they look a little bit like polar bear cubs. Harp seals can grow to four hundred pounds—almost half the average size of an adult male polar bear. Imagine a cheeseburger that weighs half as much as you do!

Baby harp seal

Ribbon seal

Polar bears hunt for seals from the edge of the ice. Seals live both on the ice and in the water. When a seal swims up to an opening in the ice—a breathing hole—the polar bear gets a chance to pounce.

Eating is a messy affair for polar bears. Their prey is wet and bloody, so bears like to clean off after a meal. They take a swim to wash their fur and keep it from getting matted. Otherwise, their fur wouldn't keep them as warm. After a bath, it's naptime. Polar bears sleep for about eight hours a day, just like humans do.

Most polar bears wander for hundreds of miles to find food. In spring, they mate. But female bears can only have babies if they are fat enough. In the fall, a pregnant polar bear builds a den where she'll give birth and live for the winter. She stays in the den for four to six months, taking care of her cubs. The babies survive on their mother's milk. But the mother bear has nothing to eat or drink the whole time she's in the den!

Another furry white animal found in the Arctic is the Arctic fox. With thick white fur, they blend into the landscape, making it easy for them to sneak up on their prey. Arctic foxes will eat anything—berries, birds' eggs, small animals, fish, or leftovers from a dead animal that a polar bear killed. Arctic foxes are small—about the size of a miniature poodle.

One of the largest animals in the Arctic is the walrus. Walrus babies weigh more than a hundred pounds when they're born, and males grow up to weigh as much as two tons! That's as much as a minivan weighs! Adults can be more than ten feet long. Walruses have two enormous teeth, called tusks. They use them to break holes in the ice. Walruses swim underwater, looking for clams and sea creatures to eat, then come up to the surface to breathe. They also use their tusks to fight off predators and to pull themselves up onto the ice.

The very biggest animals living in the Arctic are whales. The Antarctic blue whale, which can travel to the Arctic in the summer, weighs some two hundred tons—as much as thirty-three elephants! Bowhead whales can break through sea ice with their powerful heads and bodies,

even when the ice is seven inches thick. They are so strong, they can leap entirely out of the water. Bowheads grow to sixty feet long—about the length of two midsize school buses. They weigh up to two hundred thousand pounds. Some bowhead whales have lived to be two hundred years old.

Birds can be seen in the Arctic, mostly in the summer. Bald eagles, snow geese, peregrine falcons, and hundreds of other birds are regular visitors. In winter, the Arctic is too cold for most birds. Only a few are seen year-round, including snowy owls. They change colors to blend in with the landscape, turning from brown and gray in the summer to pure white in the winter.

Many of these beautiful Arctic animals would be among the dazzling surprises that Robert Peary found when he began to search for the North Pole.

CHAPTER 4
A Bitter Rivalry Begins

By the late 1800s, many explorers from England and Europe had tried to reach the North Pole—and failed. So the North Pole remained one of the last places on earth that an explorer could conquer.

Robert Peary not only wanted the fame that would come with reaching the North Pole, he also was determined to take all the credit for it.

In 1891, Peary was an officer and an engineer in the US Navy. He had sailed to South America as part of his job. And he had sailed to Greenland once. Now he was ready for his first real trip to explore the Arctic.

With money from rich donors—and with the navy giving him a paid leave—he hired a ship.

Then he recruited several men to come along. One of them was a young doctor from Brooklyn, New York, named Frederick Cook. Cook was a handsome, friendly, capable man with brown hair and bright eyes. He was well-liked wherever he went, and was eager for adventure.

Peary hired Cook to take care of anyone who got injured or sick on the journey. Cook was also assigned to learn about the Indigenous people they would meet in the north.

Frederick Cook

Before the ship even reached northern Greenland, Peary's leg was broken in an accident on the ship. Luckily, Cook was there to set the bone. Peary would not be able to walk for a whole month.

The ship sailed on until it hit ice and couldn't go any farther. Then, as planned, it turned around to go home, leaving Peary, Cook, and four men behind. With a broken leg, Peary was carried off the ship on a plank. One of the other men was Matthew Henson, a Black man who was Robert Peary's valet. Peary's wife, Josephine, was along on the trip, too.

Josephine and the men set up camp. They all lived together in a small two-room house they built with wood they'd brought along. Then they spent the winter on the cold, isolated coast of Greenland. They would need the winter months to prepare for the long trek to the pole. In spring, with everything ready, it would be time to explore.

Over the winter, Dr. Cook did everything Peary asked, proving himself to be a hard worker and quick learner.

While Peary rested in bed, he told Cook to contact the Indigenous people. Cook did, and befriended the Inuit. From them, he learned everything about how to survive in the terrible freezing cold. He learned how to hunt, fish, build igloos, and drive a dogsled.

Soon, Cook learned the Inuit language, too. Once he understood what people were saying, he could ask them to help—and he could answer their questions. They asked an important question about Josephine: Was this person a man or a woman? They couldn't tell! They had never seen anyone dressed the way American women did.

Cook gained the Inuits' trust. The Inuit were friendly and cooperative. They made fur clothing for Cook and the other men in Peary's group. They made fur boots and sleeping bags, too. They shared their sled dogs and helped the Americans build sleds. The Inuit were willing to work hard in exchange for things they valued highly—knives, matches, needles, guns, and old pieces of iron.

They had almost no source of metal to make tools. Their needles were made from animal bones.

Still, when asked, the Inuit refused to come along with Peary and his men who were ready to start walking inland. The Inuit knew that the icy interior of Greenland was dangerous, and they thought it was full of evil spirits. They believed that no one ever came back from the land Peary wanted to explore.

So Peary, Cook, and two other men set out alone across the vast empty island. Through snows and storms, they marched for days, walking 130 miles. Then all of a sudden, Peary decided to send Cook and a man named Longdon Gibson back to camp. Only one man—a Norwegian skier named Eivind Astrup—was allowed to go with him as he pushed onward. Cook was disappointed. He had come so far! He wanted to be part of the entire exploration. Yet he obeyed Peary's orders.

Why did Peary do this? Remember that he
was determined to be the only person who would
claim to have found the North Pole. He had

already made Cook and the crew promise not to write a book about the Arctic trip until a year after Peary wrote his own.

At the time, nearly everyone thought Greenland might lead straight to the North Pole. But they were wrong. Even the northernmost part of Greenland was a long way from the pole. When Peary realized this, he had to turn around. He had discovered that Greenland was an island that ended well short of the pole, but knew he would not be able to go any farther on this journey.

It would take many more trips to the Arctic before Peary came close to reaching his dream. Meanwhile, Frederick Cook began to harbor his own hopes of reaching the North Pole. And he wanted to succeed on his own, without Robert Peary.

CHAPTER 5
Cook's Adventures

Peary traveled all over the United States giving talks about the Indigenous people of Greenland. He raised a lot of money for his next expedition in the process. Cook wanted to do the same. But Peary wouldn't let him—even though Cook knew more about the Inuit than Peary did! Cook had learned the Inuit language. Peary could speak only a few words. And Peary was using Cook's notes about the Inuit people in his speeches. To Cook, it didn't seem fair.

So Cook decided to explore the topmost part of the world on his own. In the summer of 1893, he led a group of students to the northwestern coast of Greenland. Along the way, he traded with the Inuit. He gave them tools in exchange for six Inuit dogs that he wanted to bring home with him.

The Word *Eskimo*

In the past, all Indigenous people in the Arctic were called Eskimos by Americans, the British, and other outsiders. The word *eskimo* probably means "someone who makes snowshoes." Today, we use the names that Indigenous people call themselves.

Cook respected the Inuit. He knew he had to rely on their help if he ever wanted to reach the North Pole.

When he wasn't traveling, Cook returned to his doctor's office in Brooklyn. But he became bored. So in 1897, Cook set sail again, but this time for Antarctica, where the South Pole is located. Like the North Pole, it was one of the few remaining unexplored places on earth. Unlike the Arctic Circle, no human beings lived there.

Cannibalism in the Arctic

John Franklin

In 1845, a British explorer named John Franklin went looking for a way to sail from the Atlantic to the Pacific through Arctic waters. He hoped to find the route called the Northwest Passage. His two ships became stuck solid in ice as it froze around them, and remained so for more than a year and a half! In the awful cold, twenty-four of the men, including Franklin, died. The rest left the ships on April 22, 1848, in an attempt to escape the Arctic on foot. It is believed that, starving and desperate, they wound up eating their friends who had died! Ultimately, none of the men made it home alive.

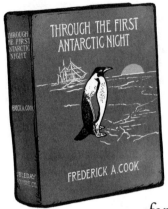

As before, Cook was hired to be the doctor onboard a ship. When the trip to Antarctica was over, Cook wrote a book about it. He also went on a lecture tour. He was famous as the only American at the time to have explored both the Arctic and Antarctic.

But Cook was modest and soft-spoken. He didn't brag about his adventures. He just was eager for whatever came next.

And the next adventure was a surprising one. Cook was asked to sail north to find an explorer who had disappeared—Robert Peary!

Peary had been gone thirty months, and seemed to be lost somewhere in the frozen Arctic.

CHAPTER 6
Saving Robert Peary

In 1898, Peary had returned by ship to Greenland and set up camp. Matthew Henson was with him, as was another doctor who had come along on the trip. For more than two years, no one had heard from him. Peary's friends and supporters—the rich men who had paid for Peary's trips—were worried. They asked Frederick Cook to join a search party in 1901 to help find the lost explorer.

Cook agreed to go, asking for no pay. He was a doctor, after all, and this was a rescue mission. When he reached Etah, a small settlement on the coast of Greenland, he found Josephine Peary there. She had arrived by ship a year earlier to search for her husband. Cook was surprised to learn that Josephine had found Peary. No one back in New York had known it. Letters could take months or even years to arrive by boat from the Arctic Circle to the United States.

Peary was now resting comfortably on the ship Josephine had come on. It was anchored near Etah. But Peary was a broken man—both

physically and emotionally. Josephine asked Dr. Cook to examine her husband, and Cook was shocked at what he saw. Peary had lost weight. His skin was leathery—a strange gray-green color. His teeth were rotten, his heart and his lungs weren't normal, and he couldn't digest his food. He wasn't even hungry most of the time. He was also suffering from night blindness.

Cook said that most of Peary's problems were due to his diet. He needed to eat raw meat, like the Inuit did. But Peary refused.

Most disabling were Peary's feet. He had lost eight of his toes from frostbite! Some had snapped off all by themselves. Others had been amputated by a doctor. He could barely walk.

Peary's health wasn't the only startling news. Josephine learned that while her husband was in the Arctic, he had taken a new wife—an Inuit wife. They had a child together. All Josephine could do was accept it.

Robert Peary's Inuit wife, Ahlikahsingwah

Josephine wanted her husband to sail home with her. Even in his condition, he wouldn't. He was

Frostbite

Frostbite can destroy fingers, toes, and other body parts if they are exposed to extremely cold temperatures. People sometimes get frostbite on their ears, nose, cheeks, and chin, too. Even with thick clothing like coats, hats, and gloves, a person's skin and the flesh can freeze to the point where they are permanently damaged.

The only way Peary could reach the North Pole was by riding on a sled—something explorers almost never did. The sleds were used to haul food and supplies for long trips. The sled's driver stood on the back edge, holding reins that were tied to the dogs. But Peary couldn't even stand on the back of a sled to drive it.

determined to stay in the Arctic another year and try again to reach the North Pole. So Josephine sailed home with a bitter heart. She had never been as important to him as his desire for fame and glory.

CHAPTER 7
Top of the World

Peary and Cook were both eager to try one last time to reach the top of the world. Not, however, together. They each decided—separately—to make one final race for the pole. The men were rivals of a sort by now. Peary thought he alone had a right to reach the North Pole. Cook thought the pole was fair game for anyone who could get there. It would be Peary's fourth attempt at seeking the pole. Cook had never tried it on his own.

In July 1907, Cook sailed north with some men who wanted to hunt in the Arctic. Only one of them—Rudolph Franke—would stay with Cook as he searched for the pole. The rest would sail home. As always, Cook would recruit Inuit to come along on the long trek.

Cook was a year ahead of Peary, who wouldn't be able to leave until 1908.

Cook had a plan for how to succeed this time. He would do things differently from Peary. For one thing, he would take fewer men along on the last, hardest part of the trip. That way, they could move faster. With fewer mouths to feed, they wouldn't have to hunt as much. They would need to build only one igloo each day to keep everybody warm. They could bring fewer supplies on the sleds, making them easier to drive. The sleds themselves would weigh half as much as Peary's. Cook had learned how to build lightweight sleds when he was a child.

Cook also planned to use the special amber-colored goggles he had invented for mountain climbing in the Arctic. That way, no one would get snow blindness.

Cook had one other very clever plan, too. He brought a collapsible boat with him. Pieces of the boat were built into one of the sleds. The sled could be taken apart and made into a boat, when needed.

If the ice broke up, Cook would never be stranded. He would be able to cross the water to reach the North Pole. And he would be able to get home again.

In August 1907, Cook arrived at Etah and then moved just a little farther north, to Annoatok. There he built a crude house for the winter. Over the next months, he and his Inuit friends prepared for the march north. They hunted for meat and made fur clothing for the trip. When spring came in 1908, they were ready.

Cook knew he would be gone for at least three months, so he needed a lot of food. For the first part of the trip, he brought eleven sleds carrying four thousand pounds of supplies. That included a thousand pounds of pemmican— a mixture of animal fat, dried meat, and berries. Pemmican was their main food every single day. The men and the dogs ate the same thing. Cook also brought twenty-five pounds of sugar, sixty pounds of biscuits, tea, coffee, wood alcohol, and matches. He needed 103 dogs to pull the sleds. Ten men came along with Cook—nine Inuit and Rudolph Franke.

Pemmican

Marching for months in the Arctic was always dangerous. Explorers often sent men out ahead, with supplies to be left in the snow. Sometimes

it was hard to find the stash of supplies when they needed it. It was also hard to stay on course, heading north, because the ice they were marching on was always drifting!

When Cook and his friends had walked four hundred miles, it turned out they had only gone two hundred miles north. The reason was that sometimes it felt as though they were wandering in circles! But at last they reached the end of solid land. Cook decided to send Franke back to camp at Annoatok. He told Franke to guard the small wooden house. It was filled with valuable things—furs, walrus tusks—as well as supplies that Cook would need when he returned. Cook also sent most of the Inuit back with Franke. He wanted only the two strongest, most loyal young men with him. They were named Etukishook and Ahwelah. Cook knew he could count on them to help him survive. In payment, he promised to give each of them a gun and a knife.

Etukishook and Ahwelah

For the next thirty-four days, Cook and his two Inuit friends walked north in the freezing cold. When food ran low, they killed a few of the dogs and fed them to the other dogs. As they neared the pole, the young Inuit men became afraid. Why was the sun never rising in the sky? Why did it stay in the same place all day? Etukishook and Ahwelah thought they were lost in a strange unnatural world. Nothing made sense. They wanted to go home, but Cook convinced them to press on.

Compasses: How to Find the North Pole

A compass is a tool that helps people know in what direction they're heading. The needle or pointer in a compass will always point north. Why? Because the small metal needle that spins inside a compass is a magnet. And the spinning of the earth around the north and south poles creates a magnetic field. It attracts the needle of a compass the same way magnets attract each other.

But does the compass point toward "true north"—the North Pole? No. The needle always points to something called "magnetic north." Magnetic north isn't right at the North Pole. It's a slowly moving spot near the North Pole where the magnetic forces come together. When Cook and Peary searched for the North Pole, they had to adjust their compass readings to find the true North Pole itself.

Finally, on April 21, 1908, Cook believed they had reached the North Pole.

At last!

It was the dream of a lifetime. Cook took measurements to make sure they had reached the North Pole—the ninetieth latitude. Then he left a note in a brass tube to prove he had been there. He had to warm the paper and pencil over a candle before he could write his note. In such cold temperatures, pencils would barely leave a mark. The note included the date, the latitude, and some details about their long trip.

Cook had reached his destination . . . but the hard part of the journey was just beginning.

Latitude

The Arctic Circle and the equator are latitude lines. They are imaginary lines drawn on the globe. They were invented as a way of dividing the globe into equal parts so that people could talk about where they were—how far north or south. Latitude lines are numbered from zero to ninety degrees. (The word *degrees* doesn't mean temperature here. It's a measurement.) At the equator, the latitude is 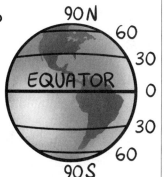 zero. At the North Pole, the latitude is ninety degrees.

When Peary and Cook were searching for the North Pole, the only way to be sure they had reached it was to take a measurement. It had to read ninety degrees. After all, there would be no sign at the North Pole, telling them they had arrived!

It would take almost a year for Cook to find his way back to Annoatok. He and the two Inuit got lost because the ice they were on was drifting and breaking apart. They used the collapsible boat many times, but still they drifted in the wrong direction. Unable to find their way home, they spent four long dark winter months in an ice cave. The only food they had was the meat of musk

oxen they had hunted before the sun disappeared.

When the sun finally came out in the spring, they set off again. But their food was now gone. Starving, they cut up pieces of a coat made from walrus hide. They boiled it. That was dinner. Another time, they ate a wax candle with cups of hot water. They even ate their shoelaces and pieces of their boots!

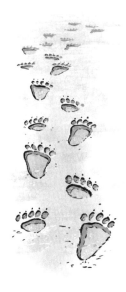

Finally, they saw something that could mean either life or death. Bear tracks! A polar bear was somewhere nearby, very likely hungry. If Cook and his friends didn't kill the bear, the bear would kill them.

So the three men set a kind of trap for the bear. They built an igloo. Then they propped up a fake seal outside, made of furs and skins, to tempt the bear. They waited inside the igloo and watched through a peephole for the bear to arrive.

When the bear came, Etukishook and Ahwelah ran out and stabbed it with a harpoon and a lance. Cook had only four cartridges, or bullets, to use in his rifle. He tossed the gun to an Inuit, who shot the bear. As fast as they could, they sliced up pieces of raw meat from the dead animal and ate hungrily. Killing the beautiful white polar bear had saved their lives.

When Cook finally reached Annoatok, it was April 1909. He said that, against all odds, he had walked to the North Pole, the first man to reach it. Then he had wandered in the Arctic for a whole year before finally returning to his camp.

He would soon find out that Robert Peary was on his way to the North Pole himself at that very moment. And Peary had no intention of letting Cook claim the victory that Peary had sought his entire life.

CHAPTER 8
Dash to the Pole

As soon as Robert Peary had heard that Cook was headed for the North Pole, he grew furious. He and his friends started to talk publicly against Cook. Peary told the *New York Times* that Cook was wrong to use "his" Inuits in the Arctic. Peary acted as if the Inuit people belonged to him!

Peary reached Etah, Greenland, in August 1908. As always, he would have to wait for spring the next year before he could set off on the final journey toward the pole. He didn't know that Cook had already beaten him to the pole—and was still alive. Everyone thought he might be dead.

Over the next year, Peary did everything he could to ruin Cook's chances of getting credit for reaching the North Pole. Peary wrote letters back to the United States. He told everyone not to believe Cook if he claimed success.

Peary also took Cook's things and kept them for himself. Cook's friend, Franke, had been guarding the precious supplies—food, furs, and ivory—in the little wooden house in Annoatok. But Franke was sick and starving. He could barely walk. He wanted to sail home. Peary wouldn't let Franke sail home on his ship unless Franke agreed to hand over all of Cook's possessions.

Peary then put a sign on the door of Cook's small house. The sign said, "Dr. Cook is long ago dead and there is no use to search for him." Peary put his own men in charge of the supply house. He told his men that if Cook showed up and needed food, he would have to pay for it!

Unable to walk for long distances, Peary faced a brutal trip to the pole. He left on February 22, 1909. He, Matthew Henson, and twenty-four men marched through blinding snowstorms in temperatures that reached fifty degrees below zero. For most of the trip, Peary rode on a fur-lined sled. As he got closer, he ordered the white men to turn around and go back to Annoatok so that he would be alone in reaching the pole. Peary still had 134 miles to go.

At this point, Matthew Henson was still with Peary. But Henson didn't know how to measure latitude. When Peary said they had reached the North Pole on April 6, 1909, Henson took his word for it.

By the time Peary returned to his camp at Etah, Frederick Cook had already returned and told people about his own trip. Cook then hiked down the coast of Greenland to a town. The trip took several weeks.

Soon, Cook announced his triumph to the world. He sent a telegram to the *New York Herald*, telling the paper he had reached the North Pole. At first, the public went crazy. Newspapers around the world wrote about him. Parties were given in his honor.

A few days later, Robert Peary raced to tell the world a different story. Peary and his powerful friends insisted that Frederick Cook was lying. Peary claimed he talked to Cook's companions, Etukishook and Ahwelah, and that they said Cook hadn't reached the pole. But Peary didn't speak their language. So how could he understand anything they said?

Then Peary pulled the meanest trick of all.

He demanded that Cook show everyone his papers, notebooks, and measuring instruments that he used on his trip to the pole. But Peary knew very well that Cook couldn't do that. Cook's papers were buried somewhere in the snow in Greenland. How did Peary know? When Peary returned from his own trip to the pole, he found a man named Harry Whitney waiting at Etah. Whitney wanted to sail home on Peary's ship. But there was a hitch. Whitney had promised to take care of Cook's things for him. He was to bring Cook's box of papers back to New York. Peary refused to let Whitney sail home unless he left all Cook's precious boxes behind— buried in the snow and ice.

In September 1909, two rival newspapers printed two different stories. The *New York Herald* wrote that Cook had discovered the North Pole. Five days later, the *New York Times* wrote that Peary had reached the pole first.

At first, most people believed Dr. Cook. But in the end, Peary's friends were richer and more powerful. They spread fake news about Cook and hurt his reputation.

For many years, Peary was given credit for being first to reach the North Pole. Today, the truth remains unclear. Some people question whether Cook reached the exact spot—even though Cook was an honest person. Others think Peary lied about his location. And even if Peary did reach the North Pole, it is Matthew Henson who deserves credit for being the first man there. Matthew had gone out ahead of Peary, leading the way that morning.

Did either man actually reach the North Pole?

The truth may remain forever buried in some boxes in the snow.

Or maybe those boxes will be found sooner than anyone previously imagined—because the Arctic snows are melting at an alarming rate.

Matthew Henson

CHAPTER 9
A Melting World

The air around our planet is getting warmer. Scientists agree that climate change is caused by human activity. We burn all kinds of fuels that put a gas called carbon dioxide into the air. The gas creates a "greenhouse effect." It traps heat around the earth the way the glass in a greenhouse traps warmth from the sun.

As the planet gets warmer, the Arctic ice is melting. In the past, some of the sea ice would melt every summer—but not all of it. Now, scientists are worried that the summer sea ice will melt completely by the year 2040. The Arctic is getting warm faster than the rest of the planet. That's bad because the ice is actually protecting us from global warming. How? The white ice reflects the sun's harsh rays away from the earth. If the ice disappears, the "reflector" will be gone. Instead, we'll just have the darker ocean water, which absorbs the sun's heat—pulling it toward the earth.

So it's a vicious circle. The more the ice melts, the warmer the planet becomes. And the warmer the planet gets, the faster the ice melts! It's what scientists call a feedback loop—a cycle that keeps happening.

Melting sea ice is bad for wildlife. Polar bears hunt for seals from the edge of the ice. When it's gone, they can't hunt as well, so they can't store up enough fat for the winter. Other animals and fish move farther north when the sea ice melts. They need colder water to survive. That's not good for fishermen, who will have to go much farther north to catch the fish. When the animals leave, the Inuit people will have fewer sources of furs and food.

Melting sea ice is bad enough. But think about what would happen if the entire ice sheet on Greenland melted. The sea level would rise by twenty feet! All the streets in New York City would be underwater. Only the tops of tall buildings, like the Empire State Building, would show. The same would happen to cities along coastlines all over the world.

The only way to save the North Pole—and the planet—is for people to stop putting so much carbon dioxide into the air. That means we have to rely on cleaner ways to make electricity and to heat our buildings. We need better ways to power

our cars and other vehicles. If we don't do those
things, the earth—and the sparkling, icy world of
the North Pole—may look very different in the
not-too-distant future.

Timeline of the North Pole

1050 CE	Ancestors of the Inuit arrive in the Arctic Circle
1845	John Franklin tries to find the Northwest Passage
1891	Robert Peary and Frederick Cook make first trip together to explore the Arctic
1898	Peary begins another exploration of the Arctic and search for the North Pole
1901	Cook agrees to search for Peary, who's been missing for almost three years
1907	Cook sails to Greenland in August to prepare for his own search for the pole
1908	Cook begins to march north in spring and reaches the North Pole on April 21
	In August, Peary arrives in Greenland, planning his final attempt at the pole
1909	Peary reaches the pole on April 6
	On September 2, the *New York Herald* announces Cook has reached the North Pole
	On September 7, the *New York Times* announces Peary has reached the North Pole
2040	Scientists predict summer sea ice will melt completely by this date

Timeline of the World

1845 — Texas becomes a US state

1880 — Thomas Edison patents his practical lightbulb

1890 — Battle of Wounded Knee, in which as many as three hundred Native Americans are killed by the US Army

1891 — First movie ever shown in the United States; it is three seconds long

1895 — X-rays are discovered

1898 — Scientist Nikola Tesla invents remote radio control

1901 — Louis Armstrong, famous jazz trumpeter, is born

1903 — The Wright brothers fly the first power-driven airplane

1906 — Earthquake in San Francisco destroys most of the city

1908 — Henry Ford builds first affordable car, the Ford Model T

1912 — The RMS *Titanic* sinks in the Atlantic Ocean after it strikes an iceberg

Bibliography

"Arctic Indigenous Peoples." *Arctic Centre, University of Lapland.* https://www.arcticcentre.org/EN/arcticregion/ Arctic-Indigenous-Peoples.

Cook, Dr. Frederick A. *My Attainment of the Pole*. New York: Cooper Square Press, 2001.

Evans, Andrew. "Is Iceland Really Green and Greenland Really Icy?" *National Geographic* (June 30, 2016), https://www. nationalgeographic.com/science/article/iceland-greenland-name-swap.

Henderson, Bruce. *True North: Peary, Cook, and the Race to the Pole*. New York: W.W. Norton & Company, 2005.

"Inuit Art History." *Nanook Inuit Art.* https://nanooq.ca/history-inuit-art/.

Smithsonian Ocean Portal. "Climate Change at the Poles." *Ocean: Find Your Blue.* September, 2011. https://ocean.si.edu/ocean-life/marine-mammals/climate-change-poles.

Turner, Gillian. *North Pole, South Pole. The Epic Quest to Solve the Great Mystery of Earth's Magnetism*. New York: The Experiment, 2010.

Wallace, Sandra Neil, and Rich Wallace. *Bound by Ice*. Honesdale, PA: Calkins Creek, 2017.

World Wildlife Fund. "Species: Polar Bear." *Protecting Wildlife for a Healthy Planet.* https://www.worldwildlife.org/species/polar-bear.